Seasons in Beulah Land

BILLY BLACKMAN

Copyright © 2011 Billy Blackman

All rights reserved.

ISBN-13:
978-1463624576

ISBN-10:
1463624573

INTRODUCTION

I guess the best place to start this book is to tell you a little about myself. I've sold Grit papers at a nickel profit each and mowed grass with a mower that had a severe smoking problem and wheezed and coughed more than it ran or cut. I've climbed cypress trees growing in "Dead Lakes," pulling Spanish moss filled with American bats and loading it into flat-bottomed boats to be paddled ashore and the moss used as worm-bed filler.

I was hired once to dig the top from an occupied grave.

I've cut pulpwood for $1 a cord (1,600 pounds) with a chainsaw and have the scars on my knees to prove it, and I've loaded wagons with hay for $1 a day. I also have shoveled cow manure (people say this qualifies me for public office) and was the mayor of Wewahitchka for a Halloween night.

I've sold fishing tackle and candy, nailed on shingles and rented horses to tourists in Orlando, and, once, had a job picking figs but was fired—the boss said, "Ye put two figs in your mouth for every one you put in your bucket."

One time my job was counting worms brought in lard cans to the fish camp where I worked, each can filled with red sawdust and that sawdust brimming with worms. My job was to sort the worms into 100 count piles to be crammed in paper cups and sold to fishermen.

Even now, memory always threatens to kick appetite out the door when I see a plate of spaghetti that looks as if it might size up to a 100 count.

I've built rocking horses and barns and grandfather clocks, and I've built railroads with a nine-pound hammer and nine pounds of sweat. I've operated road-building machinery and have leaned on a shovel or two.

I've played in gospel groups to drive souls to Christianity and played in honkey-tonks to drive people to drink, and once was the official "fishing forecaster" at the bait house where I worked. My duty was to throw a handful of crickets into the pond while prospective customers (usually from Michigan) watched. "Check'n to see if the fish are bit'n," I'd say.

The crickets would barely touch the surface before the water would boil and churn and splash as brim and bass and catfish (all veterans of hundreds of these performances) would put on their show.

During intermission those customers would always run back to the bait house, wallets in hand, lining up to buy another 100-count box of wigglers and to rent a boat and motor so they might get on the lake and not miss the road version of the house act they'd just witnessed.

I've picked cotton and stacked peanuts for pay that wouldn't cover the cost of a cheap shirt or a small jar of peanut butter and once had a job that would've been a pyromaniac's fantasy turn reality—setting fire to woods and getting paid for it.

But, the most memorable of jobs was sawing logs in "Willis Swamp," in chest-deep water, where the smell of moccasins (water, not Indian) kept my breath short and a prayer mingled with it. I was working alongside a reforming alcoholic/ex-con who fell off the wagon every Friday and came to work every Monday with wagon tracks across his head and who rode a Harley-Davidson without its mufflers and who suffered from spurts of insanity, usually while holding a chainsaw. Also working there were twin, 4-foot tall Assembly-of-God preachers who were also bluegrass singers and who couldn't swim.

While on the job, the ex-con was always worried about the boss bringing his nose around to make random breath checks, and I was always worried about stepping on a snake, and the preachers were always worried about our souls and stepping off a log and drowning in what would be chest deep water to most men.

I've downed whisky from a bottle hidden underneath a greasy bucket in the back of an old truck, socializing and putting myself on the same level as this "source" I was using for a newspaper article.

These days I work as a full-time father who's moonlighting as a musician, who's moonlighting as a writer, who's moonlighting as a house-builder, who's moonlighting as a farmer, who's moonlighting as a furniture maker who's once was as a newspaper editor and now a farrier, who, every Sunday, sits in his swing on his front porch and lets out a sigh and a "whew."

SPRING

I noticed blossoms on our peach trees today—pink noses protruding into an unpredictable world. There are also green signs of life on the apple tree we planted last January. A pair of squirrels has returned from wintering at the creek to set up housekeeping above our driveway in the hollow walnut tree - a parental gesture in anticipation of their spring batch. The narcissus are showing their stuff and the buds on the Bartlett pear tree have swelled and are ready to bloom.

My wife was in her herb bed this morning (on all fours), gently raking back the hay from atop the spearmint and thyme, removing her frost-proofing so that the afternoon sun may encourage new life. Everywhere the sap is stirring.

They (trees, flowers, herbs and my wife) think that an early showing of optimism, though presumptuous, may sway Nature to join their ranks and postpone the next frost until December.

I'm just as guilty of rushing things as they are. My sap has been stirring for two months now: The garden plot has been turned and harrowed since December, waiting with open arms for longer days.

But there's just so much a person can do to a square of dirt - idle days outnumber throttled ones. Most of last January was spent thumbing through a seed catalog, drooling over exaggerated foldouts of what could happen if I planted "Hastings" seeds. I had to re-harrow my plot to relieve myself.

Three weeks ago a letter came (bulk rate) from the editor of some dirt magazine promising to make a successful farmer/gardener out of me for a small subscription price. I've always suspected offers promising to raise the dead, so a Farmer's Almanac was bought instead with the subscription money.

The almanac said that "root crops" should be planted when the "moon is in the earthly signs of Taurus or Capricorn and decreasing in light." We laid our potatoes to rest on Feb. 7 (impatiently early by most standards, which set Valentine's Day as spud day.) Our eagerness may have cost the lives of two pecks of seed potatoes because they've yet to come up.

Yesterday I re-read a report sent to me by the Florida Cooperative Extension Service on the condition of our soil — I'd gathered 20 shovelfuls a month ago, mixed them together to get an average, and sent a sample, along with $3, to Gainesville in a plain brown paper bag.

This report showed that poor harvest couldn't be blamed on the soil. That planted the cause directly on me.

With that in mind I turned in my almanac to "above ground crops" and read where February 20 was a good day to plant bush beans and sugar snaps.

So on that day I laid off 10 rows, distributed fertilizer and worked it into the soil. We were about to drop seeds when the phone rang and I had to run into the house, cuffs filled with dirt and a fist full of bush beans, to answer it.

It was a salesman (also guilty of rushing things) representing *Somewhere Gardens,* wanting to sell us a matching-set, burial plot for half-price.

I understand his method: Die one—get one free. What I can't grasp is his timing. He should call on a cold and gray midwinter day, when a man with spring on his mind has nothing better to do than to think about death. Not on a day budding in rebirth, when a man has his cuffs full of contentment, a firm grip on a fistful of new life and a heart swelled and ready to bloom.

Not long ago my wife, tired of looking at my wilting okra and my dangling modifiers, bought me two books: a "Planter's Guide" and a "Writer's Guide."

I've read them both and have found that I could probably plant a garden using points given in the writing book, or write an article using suggestions laid out in the planter's manual.

Both start with the basics — fertilization of seeds and fertilization of ideas.

The "Planter's Guide" emphasizes the importance of having a careful balance of nitrogen, phosphorus and potassium if there is to be a rich medium so seeds may take a firm toehold and establish a good start toward a freezer full of vegetables.

Fertilization of ideas comes from nose-to-nose experiences. It has always seemed that the best writers are those who aren't full-time, but, instead, those who can take off their writer's loafers and slip on a pair of wrangler's boots when corralling just the right word seems hopeless, or put on their farmer's cap — whether it fits or not — when perspective needs cultivating, or change into their carpenter's overalls when sentence structure needs some extra nails and a little bracing.

Neither do I believe that a person can honestly write about, for instance, gardening without first experiencing hoe-handle blisters, wormy corn or the satisfaction of having straight rows. A person would have trouble writing about idyllic lifestyles without first knowing the feeling of barefootedness, yellow jackets or the gentleness of non-chlorinated water. Varying experiences are what give word-stringers a good start toward a head full of potential writings or a hamper full of finished ones.

Another important part of good gardening and good writing is proper weeding.

When gardening, each plant, each row must be painstakingly worked, taking care that no grass remains to take unfair advantage of the weaker seedlings by punching them in the nose and pocketing the nutrients for itself.

Writers have to be good weeders, too— after finishing a few rows (which come in printed form), they must carefully hoe around each word, each sentence, to weed out the comma splices; do a little transplanting if a question mark sprouts at the end of their declarative row; then finish by giving it all a through raking, piling all the sand spurs that suck the strength from their work at the ends of the rows and burning them, just in case some editor happens by. There's nothing more unforgiving than an editor with your comma splice stuck in his or her big toe.

Then there's the question of collecting waste and turning it into something useful. One collection is called the compost pile, the other the wastepaper basket. One pile is made up of a combination of horse manure and an occasional pan of leftover grits, the other of crumpled balls of paper. One makes corn grow, the other makes writing ability grow, because there is but one way to learn writing, and that is to write, and to do it every day— whether the results end up in print, in an empty tomato crate under your bed, or in the trash.

Regardless of whether you're deciding if the cucumbers need soda or if the sentence needs a semicolon, there are many similarities between writing and gardening: both require preparation, fertilization and determination, so that when market day arrives people will have a product that they won't mind sinking their teeth into.

It took me two months to build my barn, not because of laziness but because money was an object - a condition requiring me to round up and build as much of the structure as possible from experienced material.

My brother had the telephone poles I needed and had them for the right price: nothing. I would've paid him twice that amount if only he'd asked.

I dug the holes and set the poles according to a plan in my head. I nailed up the barn's rafters and put on its top. Cypress slabs were nailed up for its walls. That gave it the rough-hewn outdoorsy look that I like.

My neighbor has a different opinion. He seems almost obsessed with me painting the barn. He says it's for protection, but I think it's simply the innate attraction most men have for things painted up—be it barn or blonde.

Shortly after finishing the barn, I caught my son Justin climbing the ladder that leads to the hayloft. He struggled, hand over hand, to get from where he was to where he wanted to be. But halfway up, he remembered leaving his resolve on the floor, and I had to help him down.

I knew it was only a matter of time before his quest for dizzy heights would overpower his feelings of security, which come from having two feet firmly on the ground. So I shouldered him, took him up into the loft and walked straight for the hayloft door. I stood just close enough so he could peep over the edge.

There I explained, as best I could, the laws of gravity, acceleration, velocity and collision (sudden stops). To demonstrate the impartiality of these laws, I dropped a brick over the side, hoping he would understand that these axioms of nature have the same effect on a brick as they would have on my head if I were to fall. But from his expression, I felt he suspected the only difference between that brick and my head hitting the ground would be the end result - the brick would crack!

While we were up there the sparrow flew in. She had been busy for weeks rounding up materials and ferrying them down to where she was building a nest inside a sand pail sitting upright in a milk crate hanging on the wall.

She landed on one of the hay bales and moved her head from side to side as if making a sight measurement. Then she unthreaded a strand, clamped it in her beak and darted from bale to rafter to crate to pail, where she would bend it, weave it and tie it, following a plan buried deep in her ancestry.

I figured it wouldn't be long before she started ferrying crickets and worms instead of straw. Shortly thereafter the flying lessons would begin.

She will not teach her uneasy students the aerodynamic laws of thrust, lift and drag - the whys of flying. Her lessons will be simple: stand with your beak in the wind, jump and flap and you'll go aloft, leaving behind the uncertainties of being nest-bound, relishing a breeziness that comes from soaring high.

That approach is so much easier than climbing a ladder with a little boy on your shoulders.

Spring is just as much a condition of the spirit as it is a condition of the senses. It's not only things we can hear, can smell and can see, but it's also visions of things yet realized—fantasies of warmer times ahead when people are brimming with anticipation and are intoxicated and staggering about with spring on their breaths, swaying from flower pots to garden plots, with far too much to do to sit still, but at the same time fighting the urge to lie out on the grass alongside the dog and let the sun melt away all memories of January.

I heard my first whippoorwill of the season last week. This was my signal that spring was officially underway.

That morning I was up early to start construction on a brooder in preparation for the postal arrival of a shipment of chicks we ordered from a hatchery in Iowa. (Rhode Island Red is the variety, and at a good price — cheap cheeps so to speak).

This brooder will set out by the goose pen behind the barn, near an electric outlet so the bulb in the brooder can be jolted into service on the cold nights yet to come, when all children need a mother to keep them warm—even if she is an artificial one who gets her heat from the electric co-op.

The geese are bound to see this intrusion by birds of a different feather as a chance for a noisy encounter.

But, if my plan works, they'll have their own brood to contend with and won't have time to harass these young redheads from Rhode Island.

My plan is, on our next sunny day, to drag the water-tub from the goose pen, change its water (like changing the sheets on a bed) and let it sit out until the sun has stripped all lingerings of winter from the water, then drag the tub back into the pen and wait for Nature to take Her course.

You see, geese like to copulate in water, and if they are to be fruitful and multiply, they'll want the frigidity taken out of the water—I know I would.

By lunch on the day of the brooder assembly, the smell of sawdust filled the air behind the barn: scents of new construction that mingled well with other scents of peach blooms and apple blossoms that were also under new construction.

There was a hint of another scent in the air that day, too — faint, almost like something I'd imagined. And as it floated by it had that certain sway of step that could turn the head of any part-time farmer and cause him to lose his concentration.

One look in the direction of my neighbor's house and I saw the source that had stirred my interest: my neighbor was on his tractor, busy with ground-breaking ceremonies, and the aroma of freshly plowed dirt was in the air like some exotic fragrance. It had caught the wind and was swaying past my nose, which should have been down to the business at hand instead of up in the air and sniffing.

Taking a brooder from fantasy to fact can be a slow process, especially when you're continually stopping to listen to the signals of spring—stopping in hopes of hearing the signal of splashing water coming from the goose pen, continually pausing to remove the sawdust from your nose, pausing to sniff the air for traces of new ground that cultivate fields of optimism in the spirit.

But, the main distraction was the continual stopping to run into the house every time you think you hear the telephone ringing, dropping everything in anticipation of receiving news from the postmistress that, according to her senses, your shipment from Iowa had arrived.

SUMMER

The thermometer that hangs on the shady side of the barn read 96 degrees Sunday.

* * *

I know it's early to have asterisks, but, as E.B. White once wrote, there is no better sign of hot weather than the asterisk.

Even a writer can't work very long in this heat before the sweat runs in his mind's eye, blurring his vision and demanding he stick up a set of asterisks so he can take time to cool off.

* * *

On the railroad we also had signs that told us when it was officially summer.

One sign was when a worker metaphorically called out, "I hear the bear shaking the bushes." This meant that the "bear" was lingering nearby, ready to catch some over-zealous worker who'd yet to learn the art of keeping the bear at bay on a hot day.

"Get'n bear caught" was a phrase meaning that a worker had been overcome by heat.

Where the phrase came from not even the old timers could tell me. But the old timers could and had described to me the symptoms of getting "bear caught," even before I had been through a summer railroad season and found out for myself.

Abnormal behavior was one symptom. "A bridge gang worker got too hot tot'n rails one time," told one experienced rail-worker, "and dropped his rail dogs (the tool used to carry rails by hand) and commenced to turning flips in a muddy ditch along the roadbed."

Hallucination was another symptom. "I got bear caught one time," said another, "and laid in a shade to cool' off. A buzzard lit on a fence post and got to watch'n me. Every time I'd lay my head down, he'd lean forward like he was fix'n to come over to visit me. When I raise my head back up, he'd straighten up, looking somewhat disappointed and way underfed."

But the biggest spectacle I saw was one old man, standing in a shade along the roadbed, with his pants down around his ankles, his undershorts shining in the sun. He had his shirt pulled up under his chin, exposing his belly to the breeze, trying to get rid of the summer that had accumulated inside his clothes.

This was probably the surest sign of summer along the railroad.

Some people will do anything to scare away the bear.

* * *

Around the house, we have official signs that signal the beginning of each season.

It's officially winter when the water tub on the south side of the barn freezes over to the point where the geese can't break through to do their drinking.

In spring, it's the first whippoorwill that signals the official beginning of that season.

Fall has its beginnings when my neighbor starts cutting firewood, filling the air with the sounds of splitting wood.

And summer has its sign, too.

No, it's not the calendar that lets us know when it's summer; nor is it the thermometer in a Sunday shade screaming out 97 degrees of thermology that's the official sign of hot weather.

Neither is it those days when the air is so thin that there seems not enough to divide among us; no movement at all; the only sounds are that of the locust complaining about the heat.

And it's not the sight of the geese, staggering across the yard toward their watering hole; staggering as if they'd eaten too many green pears or overindulged in the wild cherries that cover the back yard, fermenting in the July sun—but really staggering because the "bear" had taken a swipe at them.

* * *

No, it's not even writings full of asterisks that are the official signs of summer.

* * *

It's the sign I saw yesterday.

A fellow can be sure that hot weather is officially upon him when he sees a goose standing in the middle of a washtub, complaining at the top of his lungs, as if he had an asterisk stuck in his toe.

A friend overheard me saying that I needed a work-cat to rid my barn of the mice that had been helping themselves to the scratch feed and pea seed—a situation the geese and my wife found unacceptable. (We decided against scattering poison because of the long-term consequences it could have on our three-year-old inquisitor-at-large who looks like his father, as opposed to the short-term discomfort that would come from his sitting on a cat's tail.)

It's been a month now since this friend brought me his solution to my problem in a styrofoam ice chest - its lid taped shut and pocked full of air holes.

And in that month this tabby has, without gaining an ounce, gone through eight boxes of cat food. My neighbor says she needs "wormin' " and that he has the "sure far" cure for cat worms: a concoction made from sassafras bark, red clay and rain water.

Whether it was the cat's innate distrust for anything associated with "bark," or if it was the thought of red clay stuck to the roof-of her mouth, I don't know, but the whole time he was talking up his de-wormer the tabby had one of those "over my dead body, and I'm gonna take somebody with me" expressions. So I decided to stick with the fish-flavored, easy-to-swallow caplet wormers I found at the grocery store.

This kitten is the first of her clan to come live in the country, and she might have trouble adjusting. Her genes have become acquainted with central heat and air, and now they must re-adjust themselves to living in a barn where the only relief from August comes late in the afternoon when the shade from the cherry tree reaches it, and the only comfort in January is a 50-watt bulb on the north wall to keep the washing machine from freezing.

Her biggest advantage out here is that she'll probably never smell the front grill on a speeding car.

But there are things she must learn, like just how close a cat can get to a mocking bird's house before the mama bolts out the door, swearing and swooping to peck the fur from between the intruder's ears. And she'll learn too, how to avoid our neighbor when he's in his doctoring mood.

If she would stop chasing grasshoppers long enough I'd read Thoreau's *Walden* to her as a preparatory course to country living.

But she won't sit still to be read to. So the next best thing is for her to tag along with us on our afternoon walks. There she can learn to stroll instead of gallop and she'll learn to give the hay bales, stacked near the gate, a thorough spider inspection before lying on them.

She'll learn that this is a good place to be: the faint smells of horse pasture, the preciseness of a passion flower, the perkiness of a sudden breeze — compliments of an approaching thunderstorm, the appetizing sight of birds waltzing to the tempo of those distant rumblings, the exhilaration of knowing that a field mouse might be behind the next clump of grass, and the coziness of knowing that you are where you were meant to be.

After learning all this, she'll join the rest of us in wishing that we'd all found the country much sooner.

I took my first bath in government water the other night. It was brought into our house by way of pipes, machinery and men bought and paid for by my country.

It was 10 months ago when a lady representing my government drove into our yard, bringing with her a pen, a pleasant disposition, a clipboard and the appropriate forms. By signing those forms and qualifying I became a benefactor in the distribution of wealth that our country is so intent on spreading.

Households out here were called "impoverished," and the least we could have, according to our government, was a good water supply (I never would've known we were so bad off if I hadn't been told by my government).

The system has been buried, and my water pump disconnected. We've tapped in and, within hours, have taken a bath once and flushed the commode twice using water brought to us courtesy of the federal government. And this time tie-in cost us nothing, save a small charge for paperwork and the cost of water used each month.

We weren't required to hook into their supply; we had our freedom of choice. But my government did say that if we didn't do it now it would cost us $500 to do it later.

That's not twisting a man's arm, that's twisting his wallet, and I'd much rather have my arm twisted than my wallet. Besides, $500 is a lot of money to an "impoverished" household — it was a lot of money even before I found out that we were "impoverished."

Personally, I'm not against one man helping another. But, I will admit that when I stepped into the tub and turned on the water, my conscience, not wanting to be associated with me, stepped out. It wasn't fond of being washed in water brought to us via the taxation of some over-taxed, under-appreciated working-class that already has enough on its mind without having to worry about whether or not my hands are being washed in water that's up to government standards. But my conscience will get over that— resentment will give way to rationalization and prosperity will come home to roost in liquid form.

What leaves such a bad taste in my mouth (besides the chlorinated water) is government's attempt to make dependents of us all. It had a hand in bringing its water into my house, next it'll be wanting to put its hand in my septic tank.

I know it means well and has my best interest at heart. And it is convenient to never again be worried with dirt-dobbers building their houses in the pump control, shorting it out while I'm standing under the shower with a head full of shampoo. But government seems to be riding into all our daily lives on the backs of good deeds and conveniences.

Don't get me wrong, I appreciate its concern and I know better than to turn a gift faucet off.

I'm just a man who has just finished bathing in government's watery prosperity, who—for whatever reason—doesn't feel quite as clean as he did the night before after he took his bath in Blackman's water.

I went to town yesterday to buy a bag of diapers (cost: $8) for the girl, a pair of sneakers (cost: $10) for the boy and a sack of fertilizer (cost: $6) for the butter beans.

It was still early when I returned home, and I ran inside to change into my work pants (a pair with years of gardening ground into the knees), hurrying so to take the advice of Thoreau and do our work while the dew was on the ground - - work in the form of weeding.

A good deal of time is spent on your knees when you've taken on the duty of nurturer: hours spent on all fours, spoon-feeding plants until they get old enough to feed themselves; days spent pulling up coffee weeds and nut grass, because if not for regular cultivation the garden would surely return to a primitive state.

Our beans are of the running variety so I had to contrive and to construct a trellis—something solid and permanent for young hands to reach out and grab hold of.

This trellis cost $15 ($9 for the lumber and $6 for the string) and took three hours to build—and ended up looking like something a spider-under-the-influence might string together.

Now that the beans are growing, I walk the rows from time to time, lifting their leaves and dusting their undercarriage with "Malathion" (cost: $3 a bag), and once every third day I go out and wind the new growth around the cotton fiber, training the vines to climb in the right direction.

In cash, I've spent more than $25 on the bean section alone— plus hundreds of dollars in labor if I'd bought it on the open market, even at wholesale.

I have never sat down with a pencil behind my ear, one in my mouth and one in my hand, scratched my head and figured, to the penny, if gardening reaps a profit I can jingle. Profit is not why I garden.

My furrowing connects me with the earth. Through cultivation I come to better understand our plants, to adore their dependence on us and ours on them. Gardening keeps my feet on the ground and gives me something solid to stand on. I am better because of its influence and, I hope, it's better because of mine. These things I couldn't afford to buy on the open market, even at wholesale.

I finished feeding our beans yesterday around 10 a.m., then brushed the dirt from my knees and settled down to ponder an article in the "Home Economic Review" that reported it now costs $100,681 to raise a child.

This report took my breath, and I wondered—as if I had to have payment in full by the 15th—how I would dig up that much money.

After I learned the payment schedule was stretched out for 18 years, my breathing returned and I found myself disappointed at the report— disappointed because there are some things specialists just simply shouldn't stick a price tag to.

As an experienced nurturer, I realize raising things takes both time and money: Whether winding a bean vine around a cotton fiber or a young mind around a moral fiber; whether paying 12-cents a pound for fertilizer or $1.91 a pound for Cap'n Crunch. If we set it all down in a ledger, the "liabilities" column would scare the wits out of any gardener/parent.

It's just that I am always disappointed when specialists fail to realize that some things are better left unappraised; disappointed by their need to attach a dollar figure to everything.

For the sake of balancing the books, I wouldn't know where to begin appraising a steaming bowl of beans brought to a wintery table by way of the freezer, to the freezer by way of the garden, to the garden by way of soiled jeans and sweaty determination. What dollar value do I attach to memories as I sit one day in a squeaking chair in my gray disguise, rocking through my wintery years, musing of sneakers and diapers and trips to town — the priceless harvest of the growing season?

Please allow me to attempt the impossible by trying to explain to you how being a father feels to me:

Do you remember the feeling the first time you rode your bike without the training wheels; finding the prize egg at Easter; the time you brought home that finger painting and how your parents raved over it and pretended to know what it was and hung it on the living room wall; your first train set; hearing the doctor tell your mother that you wouldn't need a shot, "Just keep him home from school tomorrow"; your first backwards flip from the diving board.

The time you heard, "You can keep him, but you'll have to feed him"; your first home run; beating your uncle at checkers; the time you caught that high fly to right field that clinched the game; and the time you stole a watermelon and how good this forbidden fruit tasted?

Do you remember the first time you asked a girl to dance and she accepted and you stumbled through the ordeal without serious injury to either you or her; the first time you kissed a girl — your eyes wide open and your lips clamped shut so your heart wouldn't jump out and scare her away.

The first time you drove the car solo; your first date that wasn't a double one; the senior prom; graduation night and the summer that followed; your first job interview; your first job; your first paycheck and spending your first tax refund?

Can you remember the first time you made love with someone whom you loved; your first garden—the planting, the hoeing, the harvesting—and how good it tasted to your tongue and to your pride.

Winning the pot with a pair of deuces; sending in the last payment on the car; your wedding night; the day you found out that you were going to be a father for the first time; when you held that first born— you both feeling helpless and mystified; the time your kid came up to you and said "Daddy, I'm proud of you."

The feeling of being missed when you are away; of being alone when that's what you want to be; a glass of iced tea waiting for you when you came in from the pea patch.

Do you know the feeling of driving through Atlanta without getting lost?

And there is the unforgettable feeling of owning your own land.

What about guessing it was the "Pluto" section you parked in when you got to Disney World that morning and being right; and being told "I love you" without having to ask to be told.

You can take the sum of all these feelings and double it, then square it, then cube it, then multiply it by the number of stars in the sky, and you still will have only an inkling of what it feels like to me to be a father.

A guy approached me at the FRM store the other day and asked, "Are you that writer feller who wrote in the paper 'bout his geese?"

I nodded. Then he closed one of his eyes and took aim with the other and asked, "Is it true they make good watchdogs?"

"No other animal will go through the trouble a goose will in keeping an area patrolled," I answered.

Thinking back, I wished I'd taken time and gone into the finer details of goose ownership with this poor, unsuspecting man—to have turned up and ruffled and examined every feather so that he might know what he was getting into.

So, in case he's reading these words, and in case he did buy his geese, I've put together a characterization from experience (three years of chasing and being chased by geese) so that he may be prepared.

As a goose owner, you never wonder how your brood feels about a subject—geese are opinionated and loud and wear those opinions handily on the tips of their tongues.

They are true disciples of decibels; they possess radical thought but do so for the sole purpose of drumming up opponents so that they (geese) may argue their point.

Geese love summer rain storms and hate cold mornings when an icy trough stands between them and their drinking; they seldom are moody and always manage to speak to you, though it's always in sarcasms, innuendos and heckling tones.

I read somewhere that geese take parenting seriously, "are protective of their young, but never indulgent," but I've yet to find this out first hand. (Either we have all of the wrong sex, or we have the correct combination but one is not of the other's liking.)

Geese are totally unbiased and would just as soon flog a white man (or woman) as they would a black, yellow, red or any combination. And they despise barnyard government and its leaders telling them what to do.

This being the case, they would make superior editorialist because they have a healthy distrust for everything and everybody and take loud offense toward enemies of self-government.

As guardians, they are better than dogs because they aren't drawn from their posts by scents of proliferation that drift in from the neighbor's poodle.

If you happen to enter the "goose zone," the gander will rake his beak across the ground, as if sharpening a knife.

But don't let this scare you—stand your ground (make sure you have a stick handy) and, sometimes, the gander will back down, and you'll find that it was actually his tongue he was sharpening for battle.

Geese will call you names while you're feeding them and will make fun of your legs when you wear shorts. They are intolerant and honest, loud and continuous. Geese hate strangers with the same passion as they hate the hand that feeds them. Geese are friends to no one but do make excellent partners, provided you have mutual goals.

They will swear and show themselves in front of the preacher, but will also stand in the pathway between your house and door-to-door candidates during an election year. They are gifted at always keeping something stirred up, and they are thankless.

Geese are as beautiful as they are pugnacious, as dependable as they are militant. And, if you're not careful, they'll cause mild trouble between husband and wife.

The other morning the wife came in from doing some garden work, shoeless and demanding that I re-cage "those *geese!*" (I'd left them out the night before.)

After corralling them, I came back inside and told her they didn't like being cooped up after having the run of the yard for a night.

The wife countered by saying she could tolerate their ingratitude much better than she could their messy habits.

"Besides," she warned with her hands on her hips while looking down at my shoes, "Ingratitude won't stick to the bottoms of your shoes and be tracked into my house."

The bowel activity of a goose is, as E.B. White put it, ''legendary.''

The duties of a father go much further than the simple act of turning out a goose at night for protection, of nailing on a shingle so heads may stay dry, of keeping a sewing machine oiled or of planting a bean seed in hopes of filling empty stomachs:

There is the fine art of tree climbing to be taught, and small shoulders to be looked over while rocks are turned and their undersides explored; there is time spent listening as a growing mind sounds out each word by syllable on each page by number.

And there are tag-a-long trips to places worth finding out about— the horse pasture with its rusty fence and old shed and muscadine vines, the goose pen with its noisy inhabitants and the thrill of getting too close to the fence and retreating just in time, the barn loft with its bales of hay where a boy might lie on a summer day when the wind is from the south and makes itself known through the cracks in the boards, the woods where the ticks and blackberries and redbugs live ... trips to this enchanted place where the beaver pond is, where the longing for a quick glimpse of the pond's lone inhabitant fill each trip with quiet approaches and pumping expectation.

There are also trips to the garden to check on the progress of the watermelons and trips back to the swing where a small foot will be stuck in the air as an attempt is made to find a thorny reminder that barefoot times in the summer are not without a price.

It is the duty of a father to have hands that sometimes smell like Desitin or eyebrows that sometimes have traces of strained beets in them; it is the duty of a father to not get his dandruff up too much when the early morning sounds of Sesame Street stomp from room to room, searching until they find him with his head under the covers, and grab him and pull him out of bed by his ears; and it is his duty to know that a trip to "Toys or Else" is sometimes appropriate, but that refusing to buy a Pee Wee Herman talking doll does not make him a bad father.

It is a father's duty to keep in mind that summer vacation for children will not last forever—it'll just seem that way. It's his duty to doctor redbugs and diaper rash, ant bites and teething gums and to get up in the middle of the night to chase away a monster that decided to spend the night under a child's bed.

It is a father's duty to guess which hand the dead frog is in ... and try to be wrong, and his duty to not lose his reason when he finds his notes folded into a paper airplane that has just made a three-point landing in the commode.

And amidst all this, it is a father's duty to do his best to always try to remember what it was like to be a child.

MONDAY - The puppy ate the daisies last night; the night before he ate the gladioli. I think sometimes the wife would be glad if he were pushing up daisies instead of digging them up. She has no patience with him, not only because of his love for her flowers, but because of his love for objects in general.

Yesterday morning she found an old shoe by the door steps. She knew right away how it got there. She also knew to whom it belonged because it had a flake of cow manure on its heel and our neighbor is the only cow-owner within a puppy radius.

TUESDAY - Went to town today to pick up a bottle of "ChiggerRid" for the little boy because red bugs have colonized around his mid-section and wake up at all hours of the night to conduct the business of bugging a little boy who should be asleep and dreaming about digging in his sand pile instead of awake and digging in his belly button.

WEDNESDAY -- The wife and I wallpapered the baby's room today. Finished without much incident: only barked at one another twice. That's a 50-percent improvement over the papering of the living room.

If couples thinking about matrimony could succeed in gluing and papering a room, and emerge still on speaking terms, they could be confident in starting their holy wedlock with a good chance it wouldn't turn into unholy headlock

THURSDAY - The tractor hasn't spoken to me in a month. I've tried everything to get her chattering again: new gas, charging her battery - but all she'll do is grumble a little, and then give me the cold shoulder again.

Well, I found out today why she has been giving me the silent treatment. For two years, I'd been telling everyone that she was a 1937 Ford 9N. I was informed today that she is a 1939 model. And we all know that you can't add two years to a lady's age and expect her to stay on speaking terms with you, even if it was a mistake.

FRIDAY - It's supposed to reach 90 degrees today. The oak shade will be a popular place. As for me, I'll work on the house.

My carpentering skills are improving daily. Last week I hit my thumb with the hammer only twice and lost my religion an equal number of times.

SATURDAY—Went for a walk this morning before the world had yet to start its engines. You show me a man who doesn't crave an occasional dose of solitude and I'll show you a man who doesn't care for his own company.

SUNDAY - Spent most of the afternoon reading "Letters of E.B. White." What I wouldn't give if he were still alive. I'd walk to Maine without shoes just to speak with him. I'd swim Allen Cove in January just to see the boathouse where he wrote about his beloved "Charlotte."

Been thinking about writing his widow, Katharine, to ask if White had been a religious man. If she answers "yes," I'd need to give up carpentering if I should hope to see him someday.

With a storm brewing in the Gulf, belching its fury in all directions, I set out Monday night, armed with a pair of scissors and a roll of scotch tape, to rekindle a fire that had drawn dangerously close to going out.

My task was to repair, as best I could, my copy of author E. B. White's *One Man's Meat,* whose pages, because of many previous readings, were loose and in danger of slipping out and hiding under the couch.

I have repaired it once before, as evidenced by the raveled tape still stuck to the cover, a repair job that has long since failed in its original purpose.

E. B. White, for several years, was about the only author I read. However, over the past five years, I had started taking him for granted—so to speak—scarcely giving him a glance, confident that he would always be on the shelf waiting for me.

But books were never meant to be left alone and, like love affairs, have a tendency to weaken and fall apart when ignored.

I hope to change that, first by repairing *One Man's Meat* so it can take at least one more affair from me that I hope to rekindle by reading it at least one more time.

My bookshelves have several volumes written by White, each perfect company on rainy nights like tonight. They are sort of like an old raincoat and a pair of work shoes: comforting and warming and soothing; a cozy fit, despite their looks.

Around 9 tonight, our 7-year old, who is also now in possession of a White book, will retire to her bedroom, to await her father who is currently in the middle of reading to her White's *Charlotte's Web*.

This book was bought by me in 1988 as a gift to her brother, who has now lent it to her.

An inscription on the faded front flap reads "Christmas 1988. To Justin from his father, who is trying to kindle in his son a fire for E.B. White.—B.B."

I read that book to him several times, on such nights as tonight and was successful in striking within him a lifelong burning for White's simple approach toward viewing a complex world; a fire that may wane for short periods on dusty shelves, but will never completely burn out; a fire that will keep him secure on a night when a storm draws near, a fire to be passed on to his sister.

One day in August, my neighbor called wanting to know if I'd work at the election polls in Midway on Sept. 2.

Even though I'd never worked at a poll before, I said yes, because, after all, it was my civic duty and the least a man could do for his country during peacetime.

I attended the class required by law for election workers. It was held in the county courthouse in an idle courtroom. With its rows of wooden benches and a podium stuck up front, it reminded me of church, so I went straight for the last pew.

It's not an easy job, this overseeing a people's right to vote. Like playing horseshoes at a church picnic, there are steadfast rules to follow.

Our supervisor stood by the podium, with the bible — the 1986 Florida Poll Workers Manual— in his hand, and instructed his congregation on what was required of them and pointed out the sins to avoid.

Our polling place is a one-room square building with bars where the windows used to be. It is just big enough to hold three voting machines, three tables, seven chairs, ice chests, lunch sacks, 20 voters and seven workers.

It has neither outside lights nor bathrooms. Without lights, early voters had to stay on their toes to avoid stumbling over the azaleas.

Without bathrooms, the democratic process slowed during the course of the day while one of its workers dashed for the woods. Nature has priority over everything, even something as sacred as a people's right to choose its leaders.

My neighbor was already at the precinct when I arrived, hammering on a homemade stand that had lost its footing and fell. It was this stand's first time working at the polls, and, like myself, it was a bit weak-kneed.

I set my lunch sack in a corner and walked over to help a co-worker who was trying to nail a miniature flag to a rickety picket stand. After achieving reasonable success (the flag wasn't quite straight), we carried the stand outside and put it in a conspicuous place, just as the law instructed us to do.

It looked lonely out there in the dark, our flag, drooping from lack of a breeze. A flag needs a breeze to stir it and make it right, just as a democratic government needs voters to stir it and keep it right.

Just then, another worker walked by, balancing a homemade cake in one hand. She placed it inside on a table that had been cleared of old lumber and invited us all to help ourselves during the day as the urge hit. And during that day, I shared my ice until it ran out and others shared their tin-foil-wrapped prizes until they ran out.

So, despite political differences, there is a certain unity on Election Day among voters and workers charged with the job of keeping their hands in the business of government.

But democracy in action can drain a person. We were glad when 7 P.M. came so we could close the doors, separate the winners from the losers and tack the results on the door.

By 9 P.M., the job was finished and democracy's servants stumbled over the azaleas and went home, bone tired.

BILLY BLACKMAN

When I was growing up in Wewahitchka Florida, almost all my cousins and uncles and aunts played either a "store-bought" or a homemade musical instrument: some played guitars with rusty strings borrowed form Uncle Ed; some played the snaggle-toothed piano at the church, some even played a washtub turned upside down, one end of a rope clamped to the middle of the tub, the other end attached to a sawed-off broom handle. A notch was carved in the opposite end of the handle so it could be anchored to the bottom rim of the tub. Then a cousin would pull the handle back and forth, changing the tension and tone of the rope and tub, plucking the rope in time with the music, his three middle fingers covered with electrician tape so blisters wouldn't get in the way of his next performance.

A front porch was the closest thing to a stage we knew: that is, until our level of perfection finally reached a point where it no longer sounded like a cat fight, and we'd get to take our talents on to the next step: the church.

Every Tuesday and Thursday night, every Sunday morning and Sunday night, every revival and dinner-on-the-grounds and special sing, my cousins and I would spend in the choir at the Assembly of God Church in

Wewahitchka as part of a group of informal singers and players gathered before each service from volunteers in the congregation.

There, with my cousins with their guitars, bass players, piano players and a one-legged drummer who was a veteran of smokier surroundings, but had found "religion" and canceled his engagements at the local honky-tonk, I'd play my guitar while the choir clapped to the never-sit-still cadence of Holiness songs that had been passed down from book to book; their volume to such a level that they would outdo with raw power what the Japanese had done with transistors in the small amplifier my parents had ordered for me from the Spiegel Catalog.

Often, a song service that started inside would end up outside with the choir marching around the church, clapping and singing with their hands raised in the air; a level of excitement that had to have disturbed the neighbors who worshiped their pillows as much as the choir worshiped their songs. But the old-time songs of the Assembly of God would make even an unbeliever willing to give up a little sleep so he could watch and pat his foot from a safe distance.

That choir would sing "I'll Fly Away" for 20 minutes at a time— chorus after chorus, verse after verse, until a growing musician had tried every "lick" his cousins had taught him, and was forced to make up some new ones to fill the ruts left by redundancy.

"Some glad morning ... I'll fly away" they would sing, and I, too, would dream of the day when I'd jump on my guitar and fly away from small towns, river banks, chain saws and log trucks, just as my cousins before me had dreamed. In my mind I'd see myself before crowds that got just as excited over my music as the congregation got over theirs.

After church, the grownups would gather around us and brag on our budding musicianship, a fertilization of compliment and confidence that helped us grow and move on to the next step—much like we do now when the little girl dances to the music she hears, or the little boy wants to pluck and pull on my guitar—just like all children do as they are beginning to take those first steps.

This our children can't help but do, because our family believes, not as much from a preaching sense as from a living testimony, that music is an heirloom, something to be passed on from one generation to the next, like Grandpa's shotgun and Grandma's bonnet.

To make good on a week-old promise made to a 5-year-old boy, I spent the better part of a Sunday afternoon trotting back and forth on the red-clay road in front of our house, holding the boy by the scruff as he straddled a weaving bicycle minus its training wheels—the boy trying to learn a lesson in stability, the father trying to muster the courage to let go of his grasp.

After making the circuit several times, I decided that the boy shouldn't overdo himself on this Day of Rest, and we stopped at a place by the road where oaks have grown side by side. Their limbs weave in, out and about, furnishing a shady spot where a father might wait for his wind to catch up, while listening to the boy who has something on his mind, as always.

As with all our conversations, no matter what topic the beginning, by-the-by, we'll find ourselves bouncing around the universe, trotting back and forth between moons and planets, planets and stars, on a ship of a boy's design. (He has a yearning for space travel—a condition inherited from his father—and plans to go there some day.) The father has an interest in the boy's dreams and has settled down to live with the truth that any celestial bouncing he does will be by delegate.

I found out, through our little talk, that space travel is something the boy has given some thought to, and he has taken steps in his mind to be ready, so that when time comes for take-off, he won't be caught with his space suit down around his knees. He says he'll travel in a craft capable of light speed (a requirement for galaxy trotting), and he'll take along his television and his dog, Tadpole, who shows great interest in whatever the boy does. He'll also take along the wooden space gun I glued together for him and a copy of "Charlotte's Web" as a reminder of home.

My being the father and having an interest in his adventure, I suggested he take along a handkerchief in case he catches a cold, his thermos filled with hot soup, some stationery and a pen. And I know his mother will insist he pack his warmest sweater, because who knows how chilly it will get that far away from home—that's the way mothers are.

"I'm taking the peanut butter, too," he said.

"Why?" I questioned. "You don't even like peanut butter."

"Because when I leave for space, I want you to come with me." (He knows how much I like peanut butter sandwiches and how much I've wanted to travel to space).

"They wouldn't let me go," I said disappointedly.

"Why?"

"I'll be too old by then."

"I'll sneak you on board," he said with a determined look. "I'll hide you in the closet until we get out of sight. I'll put food and water under my space suit and sneak it to you when nobody's looking."

"That's thoughtful of you," I said. "But, I doubt if you'll remember this little planning session by the time you grow up."

"Yes, I will," he said. "I promise."

After my wind had caught up with me, we set out again—a 37-year old father holding on to the scruff of a 5-year-old's dreams; a father flattered by the boy's thoughtful promise, a boy with the scent of accomplishment on his breath, road dust-in his nostrils and space dust in his dreams, excited by the prospects of conquering his fear of bicycles without training wheels. A father making good on a promise so the boy might remember his; a boy learning to boss around his equilibrium as the first step in his training for trips to places I once called "yonder," where a young man will need a sense of balance when he's bouncing around the universe in a ship of a boy's design, trotting back and forth from moons to planets, from planets to stars, and from driver's seat to closet, where an old man will hide with peanut butter on his breath.

BILLY BLACKMAN

For the past month the gander has had designs on the goose. And for the past week his social behavior has been totally uncharacteristic in regards to her: he has been thoughtful, pleasant and charming—a complete turnaround from his cold-weather attitude.

He doesn't fool me; I know what he's up to. And if they haven't already, I expect that they'll soon perform whatever ceremony geese perform and will become Mr. and Mrs.

But, judging from his "she can't do anything wrong" posture, I think they've already honked their vows. And I suspect that's not all they've done.

I say that because the goose has been acting at odds with herself for a week, swirling about the pen as if she had some urgent task to attend to, but not knowing exactly what it was; going through periods of quiet inwardness, after which she'd run over to the hay pile, pull some feathers from her chest and mix it with the hay. Then she'd give the whole place a thorough straightening.

The gander tries to help; but, even on his best day, he only gets in the way.

The sum of these actions can add up to but one thing: goslings before summer (God save our young peas).

Being the tender of the barnyard, I think it only fitting that I build her a proper nest - a project that shouldn't require much time, materials or ingenuity: thirty minutes, a can of nails, a board or two and an armful of hay.

As far as the goslings are concerned, my Britannica doesn't go into detail about how soon after the ceremony we should expect delivery. But my guess is that I have until late May to meet this nest-building deadline.

But the goose isn't the only lady expecting around here; and the goose nest isn't the only nest to be finished by a deadline.

We're expecting, too (Sept. 21 according to the doctor). And our nest is in the form of my wife's old home place - an old but sturdy house we had moved here from Port St. Joe, about 150 miles by the mover's route.

The house was built from heart pine more than 45 years ago by my father-in-law, who, at that time, was a young father searching for somewhere to build his family's nest.

My wife was raised in that house. So, for her every cranny is filled with and every corner stacked with childhood recollections.

I've noticed that she enjoys walking through the house, tracking sawdust from room to room, stepping over handsaws and around sacks of nails, pausing from time to time to look, to touch and to muse.

The other day I found her sitting by the window in her old bedroom (to be the baby's new nursery) in quiet inwardness, up to her ankles in new lumber and old memories, rocking and looking out past the cherry tree that's so quiet and so tall, past the pecan tree that is budding and much taller than the cherry tree, on beyond the blooming peach tree awash in pink, on to the garden, which at this stage hides all its potential because it's too young to show any signs of life—a garden where new life - put there by us - lies motionless, covered and warmed and nourished and protected; to sprout forth one day to the delight and to the wonder of the tenders.

This weekend was spent working on my finicky reminiscence of the Industrial Age: my 1939 Ford tractor.

There is probably no better symbol than an old tractor for that particular Age, with its smoking and clanking and moving parts that sometime break and have to be wired back together, or even replaced.

The boy spent some of his weekend faced with problems centered around a newer Age they call Information.

With mouse, monitor and modem he can, from his rural outpost, be traveling from world to world while I steer the tractor out to pasture and travel back and forth from one end to the other dragging an aged 5-foot mower behind me. That is, until my Industrial Age contraption sputters—as it did Saturday—and we limp to the closest shade where I can work on it in relative comfort.

The boy also had to work on his machine. His INIT conflicts and my worn-out machine kept us both busy.

If there are any similarities between his new age and my old one, other than an occasional breakdown, I guess it would be those pesky bugs.

I got into a nest of them when I happened to bump into a trailer that has spent most of its summer sitting in the pasture. I had to abandon the tractor and leave it running while I ran for cover as two dozen of those bugs swarmed and searched for whomever it was that jarred their home.

The boy also had to contend with bugs in some of his computer programs. These bugs wouldn't send him running out of the house in search for cover, but they are just as troublesome if you're trying to get some work done.

It is some comparison, this Industrial Age that runs on gasoline and baling wire and this Information Age that gets its strength from electrons and people who can speak its HyperText Markup Language, and, as Ages go, it will eventually take its place in history.

But old Ages have a tendency to not want to give up.

The old Age may smoke and clank and be held together with baling wire, but it's tough and dependable and will refuse with passion and determination to give up its place in history to this newer Age that will sooner or later use its Net to corral the older Age and put it out to pasture.

AUTUMN

I was at the airport until 10 Monday night, waiting on a little girl to land from her adventure. Monday night is the time I usually spend writing my week's column for the newspaper, but as I waited, writing a column was the last item on my list of *Things to Worry About*.

The little girl had been spending a few days, along with her second-cousin, at the grandparents' house in Holmes County, Florida.

She flew in on a single engine, 4-seater, flown by her first-cousin, a trip I figured might have the tendency to frighten her, since this was her first flight and it was a little windy Monday.

When she entered the terminal her eyes were wide and bright. "Yep, it scared her," I thought while feeling relieved. "Her flying days are over."

But the first words out of her mouth were, "I LOVED IT!" She's just like her Mama!

I noticed several weeks ago how she, at the age of eight, all of a sudden had developed an addiction for high places she could reach by climbing any number of trees in our yard.

Her favorite is an old pear tree, where a third limb from the bottom calls her on a daily basis, a perch that causes her voice to rise with excitement as she views the yard from a different perspective.

Must be the same phase I went through at that age, as did the boy and probably the mother, too: a magnetism for places higher than the ground level.

"Everything looked like toys," she said about her view from 3000 feet higher than the third limb. "It made my stomach go up and down."

"I know what you mean," I said because the thought of the girl being up in an airplane made my stomach go up and down, too. What didn't help my situation was that the plane was 30 minutes late and the receptionist calling and not being able to reach them and later calling someone and saying, "We have a problem here." Thirty seconds later I found out she was talking about her computer. However, those 30 seconds did prove that, given the right circumstances, time can stand still.

It was a hard decision I had to make to let go my grip, take control over my stomach, and let her fly. Sort of the same "up and down" feeling I had in my stomach when I was forced to finally let her go after pushing her down a dirt road on a wobbling bicycle, holding onto her shoulder with one hand while guiding her with the other.

I guess the phenomenon of letting go has as much to do with parenting as does food and shelter and protection. However, being a parental duty doesn't make letting go any easier, as it seems that young'uns known last week as "the boy" and "the girl" are this week known as "young man" and "young lady," a phenomenon known to the Romans as *tempus fugit*.

But, thinking over Monday's adventure as a whole, the saddest reality to deal with is the probability that, as far as the girl is concerned, the third limb on the pear tree just won't hold the same excitement this week as it did last.

Sunday the wife and I had a wedding anniversary.

It's hard to believe that it's been 23 years since I stood up high on a platform at the front of the First Baptist Church in Port St. Joe, chin trembling, as Susan was escorted down the aisle by her father.

Both of us had never seen a mountain and dreamed of one day seeing one. So we went to the mountains on our honeymoon, a high point in both our lives.

After our week in the mountains, we moved to a rental house in Wewahitchka, Florida (Wewa for short), underneath a stand of giant camphor trees, next door to where I grew up.

At first the rent was $20 a month. But it went up to $35 after hot water was installed.

The new water heater was put inside the bathroom—which was about the same size as our bedroom—next to the bathroom door.

Water was brought to the water heater by way of a cheap, black plastic pipe. The same type pipe was used to get the hot water out.

Sometimes the black pipe would bust on the hot water side, spurting steaming water across the pathway, blocking anyone who happened to be in the bathroom at the time from getting out: that is, until all the hot water had gone and cooler water took its place and a person could dart through.

The house had a tin roof that was loud when it rained and curtains that would blow in the winter wind, even when the windows were closed. In our bedroom, quiet and cold, you could look through the cracks in the floor and see the ground.

While in Wewa I spent a lot of time standing on the porch, trying to learn to play the fiddle because I had a knack for playing stringed instruments and needed to prove it. I had almost sawed that fiddle in half and stomped a hole in the floor before I gave up. And just in time, too. "You quit just in time," a friend told me. "The cats were about to all team up to cover ya up."

After that I took up the banjo and learned to play it well enough to fool the tonkers (residents of Southern juke joints).

For Saturday night entertainment we'd go to our bedroom, turn off the lights, throw us a blanket on the floor, flop down and snuggle as we looked out the window, through a yard puddled in moonlight and watched our neighbors fight when he came home drunk and she tried to sober him up using a cornbread skillet.

We drove a '61 Dodge Valiant that had a hood that wouldn't latch, a muffler that wouldn't stay on, and a sagging ceiling you had to peep around in order to see the road.

I got the car for a good price: traded an 8-track player and eight Chet Akins tapes for it. Despite its low-life look, it got the wife back and forth to Panama City for a year while she attended hair styling school. We were still driving it three years later when we moved to St. Joe after buying the house we are living in today (eventually we had the house in St. Joe moved here to Gadsden County).

From St. Joe we went on the road playing a string of Holiday Inns in North Carolina. The wife had to leave our home in the care of tenants while we attempted to be landlords from 600 miles away.

The wife and I celebrated 13 wedding anniversaries while on the road playing, most of them from motel rooms where all the curtains and bedspreads were the same, causing me to sometimes wake up in the morning and not know exactly which town we were in. We cooked on a hotplate, kept our perishables in an ice chest and sneaked to the maid's laundry room to do our wash while every night, people at the club would tell us that our band would go far.

We played at the Grand Ole Opera in Nashville and at Tull's Bar and Grill in Jones Homestead.

As I said, I can't believe it has been 23 years. It has been a roller coaster ride.

But roller coaster rides can be fun: that is, if you have someone by your side to hold hands with.

MONDAY — Noticed today how vigorously the little girl dislikes and objects to having her diaper changed.

As many times as this procedure has been performed over the past 11 months, one would think that she would know by now that the change—like all those carried out before—would better her current situation as well as improve the atmosphere around her crib.

But, nevertheless, she resists...with both hands and both feet and both lungs she resists.

This proves a point: that the uneasiness we humans feel about change starts early in life.

I've read where analysts have taken the "fear of change when recurring in adults" and dissected it and laid its parts on a table for examination and found as its main component the "fear of failure"— a lack of confidence in one's own abilities.

To me this analysis is far too complicated and does not pin down the truth altogether.

It is because of our natural desire to be close to familiar things, and our longing for a sense of permanence, that we wrestle with change. We grab hold of whatever we can in our attempt to slow down change as it's pulling us out the door. We drag our feet even though we know change will improve our situation, muttering and groaning and rationalizing even when we know fate has sniffed our situation and knows a change is called for.

WEDNESDAY — Started the move today from our mobile to our permanent home: from our metal house sitting on rubber tires to our wooden home resting on cement blocks.

This move signals a change in our lives, a change I know will better our current conditions (in the home we won't be bothered by something always falling on our feet when we open a closet door), but a change, nevertheless, and one I meet with a hint of hesitation.

I don't believe it to be a fear of failure causing this: I know we rewired the home as called for by county code and I'm confident that the lights will continue to work and not blink or hesitate when the boy calls on them in the middle of the night in his search for a drink of water. I know we ran the plumbing downhill and in the right direction because the commode flushes without grumbling or leaving its banks.

Why this hesitation? I don't know.

It would seem to me that a man should never feel more confident with a situation than when he's in possession of a commode that will flush.

FRIDAY—I'm amazed at the number of possessions a small family can accumulate over a small number of years and pack and stack and cram into a small house trailer.

But, I'm even more amazed to find out (three boxes-full later) at the amount of stuff that can make its home on top of a small refrigerator.

The wife decided, because we were in the process of change, to let the refrigerator top become the symbol of our efforts to simplify and to bring tidiness to our lives.

So, she proclaimed that from this day forward the refrigerator top was to be designated as an "uncluttered area" and would be "off limits" to any collections.

This movement of hers brings about a change to my way of thinking—a change I resisted and objected to and argued against on the grounds that a house just didn't seem like a home without a homey kitchen, and a kitchen just didn't seem homey without something sitting atop its refrigerator.

SUNDAY — Spent our first night as a family in our home last night.

The boy got up once and stumbled down a lighted hallway to get his water from the kitchen that now seems homey even without something atop its refrigerator; the little girl still cried and resisted change.

The wife slept confident that her proclamation had taken hold and was here to stay.

And I got up early this morning, rested and at ease with this new feeling of permanence that comes from sleeping in a permanent wooden home resting atop cement blocks instead of spending the night in a mobile, metal house sitting on rubber tires.

We were awakened the other morning from a sound sleep by an unfamiliar rustling in our front yard.

Instinctively, in a move that has become routine since we moved to the country, I jumped out of bed and stumbled toward the closet where the .22 stands in a corner, loaded with ratshot, waiting for the opportunity to surprise some plundering dog.

My wife, in her logical and precise method, did what I should have done: she looked out the window to see if the outside rustling was worth such an inside clamor.

"It's only three cows," she said.

Holsteins they were, half grown, faces drawn with both a look of accomplishment because they had stumbled upon a great secret - freedom, and a look of guilt because they somehow seemed to know they weren't supposed to have found out about this secret.

"This won't take long," I thought as I tied my shoes. "I'll herd them into my neighbor's pasture until someone can lay claim to 'em."

As I neared them, with broom in hand, all three looked up, and, as if in a pre-planned move, kicked up their heels and ran off in three different directions. Around the house they ran without stopping to regroup until they had passed the barn.

I worked my way behind them again only to have them repeat themselves, only in reverse, to regroup in the front yard.

There was nothing whimsical about their determination to remain uncaught — they meant business. They weren't about to hand over this independence they'd stumbled across by way of a rotten fence post supplied to them by a handful of termites.

I'm lucky - freedom came to me by way of the consequences of birth-place; the cows are free thanks to a handful of termites. I was born on free soil; they were born in a pasture surrounded by fencing. And it doesn't matter whether a fence is made of wire, or of government sponsored suppression - a fence is a fence.

I felt some sorrow for these early morning prowlers. They were newcomers to this freedom business, and they had fallen head-over-heels for it; sorrow because I knew that by-and-by, someone would catch up with them, even though I couldn't.

But, cows were meant to be constrained - people weren't. We were meant to be free, to have elbow room.

That's when we're at our best: to be in a position to mount a soapbox as the urge strikes; to keep our opinions unbuttoned; to assemble without fear that government is behind the bushes listening.

There are tyrants who'd take this from us, despisers of freedom who keep their people hoodwinked because they know what happens when a denied people get a taste of freedom.

The cows were caught, but they'll never be the same. While penned, they'll have food, water and shelter. But they'll still hope for the return of their liberator, the termite, and they'll torment their keepers with a determination to return to feast on a freeness they'd only tasted.

They'll do this because freedom is a delicacy of the sort that if you ever get a taste of it, no matter how small, nothing short of it will ever satisfy you again.

I brought a No. 3 washtub into our living room last Thursday to begin our preparations for winter.

With one eye closed to improve aim, I lined the tub precisely with the door on our heater (experts call it a "wood stove," but since in our house we cook on a stove and back up close to a heater, I'll go against the experts and call ours a heater) so to scoop out dusty cremations of the last cold morning of our last cold season.

Because our wood heater (which doubles as a flower stand for summer arrangements) is our only source of defrosting, nothing flammable goes to waste; things that during warm weather have one purpose quickly are charged with a different purpose during cold weather: sawdust from woodworking projects, which during summer finds itself at the foot of the rose bush, is used during winter for its kindling talents; pine cones that stub toes during barefoot seasons are used during flannel seasons to warm those same toes; scrap wood from wood-working projects (such as the grandfather clock with its metered tones that warm our home 'round the clock) will find itself cooking, not in a "stove," but in a heater; a cherry tree that offered us shade during June of '88 gave us relief of a different sort during the January of '89 after it had been cut and split.

The ashes I dug from the heater last week were the last evidence of that tree. So I thought it only fitting that I dump them around the old stump where descendants of that tree now gather, so the future may grow from the past, and to ensure that summers to come will be shady and the winter of 2010 will be warm, inside the house anyway.

Though we have several varieties of trees on our property that produce sufficient BTUs, I prefer cherry because it doesn't argue with my ax during splitting time.

Traditionally, I do my wood chopping next to the goose pen, partly because of logistics (during winter a section of the pen is set aside for wood storage), but mostly just to keep the geese wondering what I'm up to.

Geese know instinctively that a block of wood and an ax have another purpose besides stocking a wood pile, especially as the holiday season approaches.

This gesture might be interpreted psychologically as animal cruelty. But I call it just plain ol' revenge toward fowl who think it's their job to nip at my back pockets when I bend over to stack firewood in preparation for nippy weather.

My ax had done nothing but hang around all summer and was out of shape for winter when the first frost came last week: the handle had dried and lost weight, allowing the head to slip like too-big-a-britches on a too-small-a-belly.

Nothing will encourage an ax user to fly off the handle more quickly than to have his ax head trying to do the same.

I pulled an old nail out of the barn wall where the ax hangs during summer (that nail won't be needed again until warm weather sets in) and drove it into the head-end of the handle, hoping the expansion might fill in the loose areas.

It didn't work.

So, following the advice of my neighbor, I took the goose tub/ash pail, filled it with water and dropped the ax head, handle and all, into the tub so the water might swell the wood.

"There's nothing like a good soaking to get an ax in shape for winter," he told me.

And it worked.

Like all good advice, I found that it carried over well into other areas as well.

After a week of cutting and measuring and splitting and stacking, with a goal in mind of three rows of 4 x 4 x 8, I've spent an equal amount of time in a tub of warm water; not the goose tub, but the bathtub; not taking a bath as is the usual purpose of sitting in a tub, but just soaking. Like my neighbor said, "There's nothing like a good soaking to get an ax," and its user, "in shape for winter."

We took our four-year-old to the fair again this year so he could have his equilibrium tossed about, and have his pockets and stomach stuffed with junk — an adventure that comes every year as summer changes to autumn, on an afternoon that goes by like lightning.

The Tallahassee fairgrounds are set up so that when you enter the main gate, rows of buildings filled with prize pullets, cakes and cattle stand between you and the midway.

For a dabbling agriculturalist, the intoxicating sight of chickens (garden varieties as well as gaudy, experimental ones) on display is hard to pass up; the thick smell of young cows and old hay is magnetic; the electric sounds of an announcer echoing across the fairgrounds the results of the cattle judging is as reviving as the first cool night of the season. The feeling of oneness between people who prefer barnyards to city streets makes dabblers feel right at home.

But for a little boy — who'd caught a glimpse of the Ferris wheel on his way in— checking the squareness of a bull isn't on his list of things to do on Fair Day.

And a boy can't be expected to sit still while the duties of chickens are explained to him, especially when there's a clown just 20 feet away, making stretchable dogs by twisting and tying balloons.

I used to enjoy the midway portion of the grounds. But I've found that after a man has a certain amount of fair seasons under his belt, he goes through a change— the thrill of being tossed and tumbled like a sock in a clothes dryer gives way to the gentler, observer side of fair goings-on.

I was lucky last year: our young adventurer was restricted, by his own choice, to ground-bound, slow spinning rides where a father could hang on and not lose his head — or his lunch.

But this year was different; his youthful desire for loftiness was one year older and the merry-go-round didn't hold the same exalted position it once had. Nature told him it was time to move on.

"Do you want to ride the toy cars?" I asked

"No," he said. "The Ferris Wheel."

Luckily, my head can still tolerate a Ferris wheel. Sitting on it, a man can be elevated right-side-up and keep his wits about himself.

So, up we went until our heads were in the clouds, two boys with nothing better to do on an autumn afternoon.

From our perch we had a birds-eye-view of everything: trees colored by the changing season; the fairgrounds with its booths of targets and toy guns and the lines of sharp-shooters waiting to prove their marksmanship by winning a stuffed trophy for their best girl; parents, once participating, but now forced by the passing seasons to watch from the ground as older kids are tossed and tumbled and turned inside out.

From up there, perched on top of the world, I looked down to the ground at a father (also on top of the world), with his shouldered child, as they made their way to the merry-go-round; and I looked next to me at the little boy squeezing my hand, the same way he squeezed it last season while we rode the merry-go-round, and I was saddened at the thought of just how quickly these fair seasons pass by - just like lightning.

My wife bought me a hammock for our wedding anniversary. I've finished hanging it between a blackjack oak and a black cherry tree and, at this moment, am taking it for a test run.

Lying here, I've noticed definite signs that winter isn't far off. Signs in the form of a vocal number of prying crows, flying around, trying to find a deserted cornfield and its owner with his back turned.

But, in retrospect, winter has been throwing hints of its approach for some time now: the horse woke us early yesterday morning - as he always does on the first cool morning after summer - trampling up and down the fence line, kicking up his heels in welcoming gesture toward cooler days; blooming dog fennels and flowering crotalaria have washed the roadside with a final stroke of fall color; okra pods are hanging around the stalks, snoozing and going to seed; collards are waiting around for the first light frost to sweeten them with its gentle touch; and the sight of my neighbor ambling toward his woodpile every morning with an ax balanced on his right shoulder.

Another sign that frost is soon expected is the sight of my wife spreading hay atop her herb bed, tucking in her spearmint so the first killing frost won't kindle in them a terminal case of pneumonia.

This is my signal that winter preparations have officially started.

Around here there are a number of things to complete if the first frost isn't to catch our place with its pants down: Pipes to re-wrap; a tractor, a truck and a car to be winterized (I always check the condition of our radiators on the morning of the horse frolics, because I've grown to trust him in keeping me advised on winter's advance. Besides, remembering to do certain chores is easier if you attach an event to them).

It's also time to grease the harrow and mower and bed them down under the shed so that they may rest through the sleepy winter without fear of losing their bearings from lack of use.

It's time to test the bulb behind the washing machine along the north wall of the barn, to make certain it'll be quick to keep that end of the barn thawed on the icy nights that are bound to come.

Tomorrow I plan to put Sevin Dust inside the seed box so bugs and mice won't have a winter-long picnic at the expense of next year's harvest.

Apart from the stirrings in the herb bed, another clear sign of impending change is the different sounds that tag along with this time of year: squirrels hustling from limb to limb, pushed by a deadline in their senses; dry leaves rustling across the yard pushed by northerly gusts of wintery intent.

But the surest sign of winter's approach is the goings-on around my neighbor's woodpile.

The distinct tone of an ax hitting and splitting a block of wood is just as sure an overture to winter as is a corn field full of noisy crows.

Isn't it interesting to note how panic sometimes can be as contagious as a head cold?

After carving our jack-o-lantern, we took the innards over to our neighbor's henhouse in a plastic bucket.

Our son, not being accustomed to how jittery chickens can be, ran up to the fence unannounced and startled a hen that was napping in the sun.

In a matter of seconds that one unsettled hen had incited a riot, and panic spread instantaneously until every resident had been shaken from her roost.

We dumped the scraps over the fence (which seemed to settle the hysteria a bit) and returned home where the boy settled down for a closer examination of the orange monster we'd created earlier with a dull knife, his imagination carving sharp images of ghosts and goblins far more realistic than any contrived by Hollywood. I settled down to read *The Invasion from Mars,* by Hadley Cantril.

This book, subtitled "A study in the psychology of panic," gets its meat from the 1938 Mercury Theatre radio broadcast of H.G. Wells' novel *War of the Worlds*. This show, narrated by Orson Welles, lasted one hour.

The show was very believable, that is until near the end when the fiction started showing through and the invading Martians died of head colds.

But by the time the truth was known, thousands of people, from Maine to California, had taken the show as the truth, panicked and were out peeping under the bushes for Martians. "The end is near," they believed.

The only previous such incident happened in England on Jan. 16, 1926, when Father Ronald Knox, during a period of labor unrest, in his usual news break, startled his listeners with the report of an unruly mob that had attempted to demolish the House of Parliament and had already brought down Big Ben with trench mortars.

Though the show is said to have been just as realistic, it didn't cause the degree of panic that the Welles' hoax did.

I think the reason for this was in the timing, and I wonder if the "Invasion" show would have been as effective if it had aired in January instead of during the Halloween season when we all may be subconsciously uneasy and a bit jumpy.

Looking back, it seems that panic has always been ripe for harvest during October: the frenzy in the chicken yard, the market crash of 1929, the "Invasion" by Welles, and the market crash of 1987, all happened in October.

We know that in ancient times, people believed that October was the last month the underworld had to afflict and inflict before the start of the holy season, that on Halloween night zombies would walk the darkened earth in the guise of macabre witches and black cats; that against this evil the only protection was light, even if the source was flickering and came from within a gutted pumpkin sitting on a fence post— a defense mechanism we'll have in place tonight.

But I know what will happen tonight: the dog (who is always uneasy after dark) will see this father-made monster flickering in the darkness, and his mind will conjure all degrees of hysteria and he will alert the neighborhood, and panic, as contagious as it is, will spread from dog to dog, up and down the road.

And there I'll be, up at all hours, slipping on my socks so as not to catch a head cold, sneaking up to the bedroom window --- peeping and wondering, because nothing sets the mood on All Hallows Eve like a neighborhood full of uneasy dogs.

WINTER

Our watch-dog-in-training woke us up before sunrise the other morning. (We have grown to depend on him to sound the alarm when a prowler is about, just as much as he has grown to depend on us to sound the alarm when it's suppertime) We peeped out the window with flashlight (which we depend on to split the darkness) in hand to see what had rattled the dog's nerves.

Beneath the fig tree is our compost pile, made up mostly of table scraps and a watermelon rind or two, plus a once-a-month scraping from the floor of the goose pen. Standing in the middle of this pile was a 'possum, helping himself to the cold peas and other items that the dog won't touch, but doesn't want anything else to touch either.

This is not the first time the 'possum has come in the darkness to feast under the tree. Like myself, the fig tree and the dog, he thrives on my wife's cooking and has grown to depend on it.

I depend on her cooking for strength enough to do the chores around here: things like propping up the pear tree limbs which have started to sag under the weight of their own talents. These limbs look to me for support in the form of boards, or whatever else I can find for bracing.

A pear tree will shed one-third of its fruit early. This is a natural thinning process that it depends on so that the ones left in the tree may have room and board enough to flourish. This makes for larger pears, which accounts for the sagging limbs.

I always pick up the pears that the tree has kicked out and feed them to the geese. This is the first step in the making of "scrapings from-the floor . . ." and after many ups and downs, the pears will eventually find themselves under the fig tree.

Another chore is mowing the field. I depend on the tractor to help with that; the tractor depends on the mechanic to keep it in tune, the mechanic depends on my hiring him and keeping him supplied in beer change. The storekeeper depends on the mechanic's beer change; I depend on the storekeeper for fuel to keep the tractor fed so it may help me with the lawn. The egrets look to the mowed field for support in the form of easy-to-spot grasshoppers; I look to the egrets to keep the grasshoppers upset enough to keep their heads lowered so they can't set their sights on my garden.

The garden depends on the horse for fertilizer; the horse waits on the corn shucks so he may feast and make more fertilizer, I depend on the vegetables to give me strength enough to carry out the table scraps at night and to clean out the goose pen once-a-month; the 'possum waits on the darkness and the dog waits on the opossum so he may jar us out of bed in the middle of the night.

The compost pile relies on decomposition and this breakdown relies on table scraps to fire it. And the fig tree depends on the compost so it, too, may have a bumper crop this summer.

This is all good, because I've grown to depend on warmed fig preserves on cold winter mornings to put the taste of summer back into my frosty heart.

SEPTEMBER 1988—Since the President is getting himself a new Air Force One* - a Boeing 747 to be used, like its predecessor, as his official taxi, and to stand ready to whisk him and other top officials off the ground during the prelude to nuclear destruction - I wonder if he would send us a new front tire (size P225/75B15) for our truck so that in the event our country is asked to step outside we would be able to run from the end of the world in a reasonably safe fashion.

Around our house we haven't talked much about the "what ifs," but we need to. Every household needs a plan - a list of "things to load in the event of war," printed on white paper and stuck to the refrigerator door by way of an elephant-shaped magnet.

The president, I'm sure, already has his bag packed and waiting on board just in case. It's probably stuffed with the bare requirements: a shaving kit, a Geiger counter, clean socks (black) and extra shirts (no starch). And hidden in a false bottom of his satchel, an unopened pack of white handkerchiefs — they can sometimes come in handy during wartime.

I can see him on that dreadful day, standing at his ship's door, looking like Noah, checking his list as people clamor to get on board. "Let me see... We've got a president and a first lady, two Secret Service men, a pilot and a copilot, and two senators and two representatives (a male and female of each).

I've packed nothing yet and doubt if I will. The back of my truck is too dirty to store a suitcase of clean clothes in anyway. I've used it too many times to haul manure to the garden or dirt to refill the old well (it always sinks in a bit after it rains).

This well, with its squared sides carved in red clay, would've been a good start toward a fallout shelter. We decided instead to fill it with dirt and plant roses in it (roses make better gestures of peace).

But I have gone as far as making a mental list of things to take: the peas we canned last summer, shoes (boots instead of slippers), aspirin in case we get the sniffles, clothes (overalls instead of dress pants). We'd need peanut butter and a hammer, a hurricane lamp and a loaf of bread, a hacksaw and the .22 rifle, the photo album and the grandfather clock, my Harper's magazine and the bug spray, a Boy Scout Manual and two dry sticks. We'd also need both beds because our 3-year old likes to sleep by himself now.

But, in these days, with the ire of warfare advanced to the point where ruination can be on top of you before you know it, I doubt if we'll have time to load anything — no time to feed the geese, no time to water the roses. So I think we'll just stay home.

Besides, the right front tire on my truck keeps leaking down, and the last thing a man needs when he's barreling out the door during a nuclear attack is to come face to face with a saggy tire, especially when he's busy trying to save his family from the end of the world!

There will be another mouth to feed around here in just a few weeks, and we are all basking in a delight of wait and wonder.

With expectation, we'd long set aside and readied a special section of our home to cradle this newcomer. And now we long for the day when it will make its presence known— a day we know to be near because we're seeing all the signs.

Although we realize there will be the cleanups and the regular feedings, the belches as well as the blessings, the special pampering, the sore back from all the swinging and the hints of regret during the wet times, we look forward to the coziness radiated by such additions, and we will warm ourselves to the bone by the sounds we'll hear as much as by the closeness we'll feel.

With two children and their arrivals under our belts, you would think this all should be routine by now, but it's not — this one is different.

You see, this new mouth to feed I speak of does not cry, nor will it make its presence known by feminine labor pains (although I've started feeling labor pains of a different sort).

This new addition, this new mouth to feed is not a baby—it's a wood heater.

For weeks, I've been storing up provisions for this new addition of ours, striking out to the woods with my ax across my shoulder like a readied gun—on a safari of sorts —in search of flammable objects.

One day I left on a trip of specific purpose, a trip in search of basic game: seasoned pine stumps called lightard.

Back and forth across the field I hunted, with my nose to the ground like a rookie hound, hunting for this special breed unlike any other, striking with my ax every log I stumbled across, stooping and grabbing and sniffing the splinters to check them for that certain scent, then throwing them down in frustration when they failed the test.

This search netted not the first seasoned splinter for my trophy case (a wooden box setting by the stove, its contents to be handy for quick starts on slow-start mornings). Our property has long been farmland where previous owners went to great trouble to rid it of most stumps.

But, I continued to hunt, the memories of winters past breathing down my neck, pushed by a reality that back home small hands would depend on my dogged persistence to keep them warm.

Then, all at once, something caught my hunter's eye: jagged, wooden antlers sticking up above the grass. There it was. The stump I'd been looking for.

A quick look around for snakes, an accurate hop over the grass, a hardy chop that hit home, and a solid sniff confirmed that I'd bagged my first seasoned kill of the season.

This stump was so "fat"—as we hunters call it—that the fumes burned my eyes. I closed them and rubbed them and could hear the sounds of a crackling fire and see visions of four small and two medium-sized hands snug in the pocket of warmth furnished by a father's duty to the people in his charge.

It wasn't long before I'd huffed and puffed (a procedure I'd learned as my wife's coach in our childbirth classes) and hacked and chopped and pulled and tugged as much of the stump as I could carry.

Then, like some wild animal with survival on its mind, I raked straw with my hands and covered the part of the stump left behind, hiding my kill for later consumption.

Back across the field I strutted with my trophy across my shoulder, it ready to be cut up into smaller pieces for easier digestion, sap dripping from the wounds I'd inflicted with my ax; a trophy any proven provider would gladly let go up the chimney and fill a blue frostbitten sky with white smoke and scents of coziness.

The Castle of St. Nicholas, Top Floor, North Pole

My Dear Justin Blackman:

I received the letter you dictated to your father.

I am so glad you have been a "good boy." But I do so hope this phenomenon is because of your nature and not because of some fear you have that I might not visit you on Christmas Eve if you fail to trim your boyish tomfoolery throughout the year.

Time has done me an injustice by handing me the condition of being one who sits at some big desk with a pencil in hand, going over a mythical list of names, checking off the children who've been "naughty." (Bring this letter real close and read silently because I'm going to reveal to you a great secret: this idea of a know-it-all Santa going over this list is simply not true. This reputation was given to me by certain parents as leverage to get children to clean up their rooms or to get to bed on time or to eat their vegetables).

But, I do want you to know that I am pleased that you have been so helpful in teaching your little sister how to laugh and how to say "ball," and teaching her that pigs don't bark and that daisies don't bite, but geese do.

And speaking of geese, I received word from your geese concerning their wishes for Christmas. They have let it be known that they want only one thing this year. They asked that when I get into your house I look on the top shelf of the book case, pull down the third book from the left entitled "Norman Rockwell's Christmas Book" and tear out page 216 because on that page "you'll find the recipe for Christmas Roast Goose." they wrote to me.

You know for sure by now, but I'd still like to confirm it: Yes! The Santa at the annual Christmas party is your father. But don't get upset, he has my permission to stuff pillows up his shirt and to glue on cotton-ball eyebrows because during the busy season I just can't take time to leave the North Pole to make personal appearances.

I knew you suspected him as early as two seasons ago when I overheard you tell your mother, "Look Mamma! Santa has on a watch just like Daddy's."

And I remember that even the year before that he was close to being found out when one little girl sitting on the front row whispered to her friend, "That's not the real Santa."

"How can you tell?" the other girl whispered back.

"Santa does not wear penny loafers."

But, if I know your Daddy, he'll continue this yearly masquerade as long as he has in his heart my permission and as long as he can be tolerated, because being found out makes no difference to him.

I'll close by putting to rest a quiet concern of yours; a worry that only you and I know of. You're afraid that because you live in a rural area with few street lights for reference, and because your mailing address is Midway, Florida, and your telephone is listed in Havana, Florida, and your house is in neither place, that I won't be able to find you on Christmas Eve night.

But, believe me when I tell you: if, when you go to sleep that night, you will dream of sleigh bells and reindeer and stuffed stockings and a jolly man who loves you; if you will dream of a world as wide and wonderful as the sky, a simpler world designed by a special architect with children in mind, a world as kind and as generous and as loving and as innocent as a 6-year-old can dream it to be—if you do this, your heart will send up a special beacon that can be seen only by me, and I will find this glowing spirit of yours nestled in the darkness of a rural Christmas.

Your Forever Loving Santa

The barn loft has been rezoned to take on a new purpose this holiday season. It's still the storehouse for old books and baby clothes; but now, because of its off-limits status to little boys, it's also Santa's new workshop.

Last Christmas we had no trouble keeping a lid on this Saint Nick affair. We kept the incriminating evidence of our involvement hidden behind some boxes under our bed, far out of reach of little hands that were apt to stumble across the truth.

This year, though, Justin thinks Santa lives at the mall and some scheming was needed or else he might discover his Santa living within earshot.

Getting the boxes of loose parts out to the barn, unseen, posed a problem for this mom and pop undertaking, especially since there wasn't an elf in sight.

And once there, the inside hatch being too small to accommodate the larger cartons, (Santa can just squeeze through it), we would have to hoist the loot up by way of a squeaky pulley and its weathered rope, which I have hooked over the hay door on a pole sticking out from the barn, pointing due North.

We solved both problems by making our deliveries after the little boy was snug in his bed, guided to our destination by a D-cell star.

Around here, Christmases have changed regularly over the past four years: the boy spent his first holiday crawling between fancy bows and sparkling ornaments; Christmas before last, my life was flooded with that "Sesame Street" bunch. By January I'd contracted a severe case of Bert-sitis, complicated by an ever-tormenting Ernie-nia; last season brought with it the "Thunder Cats," plus accessories. Have you ever settled into a warm bath after a chilling day only to be greeted by a "Willy Kat" with open arms?

This year visions of a small bicycle dance in his head, troubling his sleep.

And it looks as if Santa will make good on that promise. That is, if he's able to get his things in order in the blackness of a powerless workshop.

A lantern sits on some hay bales, looking over Santa's shoulder, splitting the darkness just enough so he can go about his business, but not enough so written instructions may enlighten him. But, during this season, instructions should be read only in desperation. Line-by-line coaching puts too much predictability into such a play-it-by-ear occasion.

The lowering of a bicycle from a hayloft at 3 a.m. on Christmas morning will be the true test of this Santa.

What worries me is that squeaky pulley. I fear that in the silence of a rural Christmas the noise will alarm the geese, and they'll siren my neighbor's dog, whose job is to keep the other dogs up and down the road posted on such matters; and that a little boy, too excited by the prospects to sleep, will be alerted by the caroling and will jump out of bed and run to the window to try and catch the magic spectacle of an incoming sleigh and its jolly pilot. And I'd be caught - rope in hand, bicycle dangling in mid-air. And the secret would be out.

Sometimes a Santa with only four-years' experience can arouse more clatter than a whole herd of prancing reindeer.

I think I might owe my neighbors an explanation, those who thought they heard a chainsaw going full blast from inside the Blackman house early Monday morning.

It all started right after Thanksgiving when we set out on our annual trip to get a Christmas tree.

The wife likes big trees. Last year we had a big tree. This year the tree was even...

Well, it took two adults to drag the tree from where I cut it down to the scales. It took two grown men to get it on top of the wife's vehicle. Once it was on top, several feet hung off the front and onto the windshield and about a foot or so extended past the back glass.

We had to pull limbs out of the way and blaze a trail through a holiday wilderness just to get inside the vehicle once the tree was tied on top.

On the way home we looked like a creeping Christmas display on four radial tires. People stared!

Once home we had to heave the tree onto the deck where I had to cut $5 worth off the top so it would stand up inside the den. All that was left to do was get it through the door.

I grabbed it by the foot and dragged it toward the door while the wife pushed. The door opening quickly filled with at least two feet of tree left over on both sides.

We bent limbs and pulled, bent and pulled until finally we got it inside. Once inside I had to trim the tree's foot so it would fit inside an extra large tree stand. Once that was finished, all I had to do was stand it up.

It couldn't be done: at least not without either an army of elves or some sort of leverage or anti-gravity device. I was able to find the leverage I needed by balancing the tree over a coffee table where I gave it a hard flip and it landed in a semi-upright position. I pushed it again and it leaned over into a corner and was able to stand on its own. That's more than I could say for myself after it was all over with.

Well, this past Monday it came time to get the crumbling remains back out the same way I had brought them in.

I took a hose and siphoned most of the water out of the tree stand. The other gallon was to end up on the floor.

But how was I to get this ghost of our Christmas Past, that had turned into a 10-foot, 150-pound, stabbing, needling porcupine, out the door without me winding up bloody and wounded and needing stitches. The answer was easy: Divide and conquer... a bunch of small porcupines are easier to handle than a giant one. I simply needed to cut it into smaller chunks that could be handled without my having green teeth buried into my fingers.

So, neighbors, you did hear what you thought you heard running inside the Blackmans' den Monday morning. A fellow needs whatever type sword he can find — even one that runs off a gas/oil mix — when he's forced to confront a flesh-eating Christmas tree.

Well, we are now completely out of the chicken business, put in this position several winter nights ago by what I figure was a *Canis latrans,* sometimes called a "barking dog," or what's better known around here as a stinkin' ol' coyote.

I shouldn't be surprised—and I'm not—at what happened, knowing that what motivates these rawboned creatures is their forever-tormenting, forever-empty stomachs. And believe me; I know that when you're hungry, nothing hits the spot like chicken. Of course, I like mine cooked a little more than the coyote does.

As I said, I'm not surprised, but I am angry and if I'd only listened to what our two watchdogs were trying to tell me that night, I would have run outside in whatever I happened to be wearing, or not wearing, at the time, shotgun in hand, and rid the Gadsden countryside of at least one pest, and maybe two.

But in all honesty, coyotes can be advantageous to an area. They eat countless numbers of crop-destroying vermin. They help control the spread of disease, and keep the air less offensive by eating carrion, like armadillos that aren't as lucky as chickens at crossing the road. Now if only the coyotes would eat the live armadillos too, I might be able to find it in my heart to forgive them for eating that last rooster of mine.

Coyotes also eat rabbits, crayfish, lizards and fruit. And it's rumored they love watermelons and are gifted enough to pick the ripe over the unripe.

As parents and teachers, coyotes rank highly, with both parents taking an active role in feeding and teaching their five to seven pups to stand on their own four feet, not to depend on the coyote society as a whole to feed them.

Coyotes conform to any environment that produces a food source, including the Blackman barnyard. They can and do live close to civilization. In fact, one was found living in downtown Los Angeles, which tells me that they might not be as intelligent as some naturalists say they are.

There's an Indian legend that says the coyote will be the last animal on Earth after all other creatures (including chickens) have vanished.

That legend sounds almost religious, which goes to show that one society's dogma can be another society's disgust, if that society happens to own chickens.

The little girl, Jillian, who is now 8, learned one of those things called Life's Lessons last week after she found a turtle in some murky water and immediately adopted it and assigned it a name: Louie.

I don't know what scientists call the variety she found, but back home we called them Stink Jims.

The girl first fixed him up nice-but-cramped living quarters in a fish bowl the boy had used in his science project.

She had about half an inch of water in the bottom and a small rock so he could get above the water line during those times when he might want his feet to dry out.

But that night the girl, who figured that a left over fish bowl from a science project wasn't quite the spacious surroundings her turtle was accustomed to, found the bottom to an old ice cream churn that would hold at least two gallons of turtles, but in this case it only had to hold one.

These larger living quarters would also protect Louie — a turtle isn't the type house guest the wife cottons to so he was going to spend the night on the porch — from Rex: a half Lab, half Boxer who will eat anything that doesn't eat him first, including Stink Jims.

She put a couple of inches of water in the bottom, placed the rock in the middle and included several chunks of raw bacon, so Louie wouldn't have to go without supper that night.

The weather wouldn't be a concern since the forecaster said it would only get down to 38 degrees that night. Louie would be cool, but not nearly as cool as the reception he would get if the wife found him sleeping under the little girl's bed.

But, as you already know, the only thing predictable about the weather forecasting business is that it can be off by a few degrees, and the temperature dropped to 30 degrees that night.

The next morning cries from the little girl echoed across the frosty front yard, cries that brought me and Rex to the front porch where the little girl was learning her Life's Lessons: never leave a turtle outside in water when there's even a chance the temperature will drop below freezing, no matter what the six o'clock report says.

"He's dead!" she cried. "I hit him on the head with a stick and he wouldn't move! He froze to death!"

Sure enough, the water, and the turtle in it, was frozen into what could be called a Swampsicle. The turtle's head was sticking out of the ice just enough for a little girl to get a good shot at it, with her life-revitalization stick.

"His eyes are like this," the little girl said as she made her eyes as wide as possible, the way they looked the first time she rode a Ferris wheel.

We left for school, the girl sobbing, the turtle still frozen inside the bucket on the porch and me trying to comfort her. I first thought that maybe dedicating a song to Louie might help, like "Freeze the Jolly Good Fellow." But I decided instead it would be better to promise the little girl that we'd scour the mud holes of Eastern Gadsden County until we found her a replacement Louie.

But, we didn't have to. When she returned from school another Life's Lesson awaited her: the sun can work miracles on an icy day.

She found the ice melted and Louie swimming around — one of the advantages of being cold blooded — as if being frozen and thawed was a routine experience for a turtle; now feeling fine, except for a probable headache from being hit on the head with a stick by a little girl trying to knock some life back into him.

We have designated one corner of our property to be our family burial plot so someday we may attach ourselves permanently to this land we already have formed such an attachment for.

This decision was not taken lightly—not the decision on home burial, but the decision of where the actual plot should be.

We considered first it being at the far end of the pasture, but ruled out that spot because that end of the property is someday to be the boy's share, and in later years when decisions are his own, he might not want that type of garden that close to his back door.

So we decided that our place of rest would be a small corner plot between the house and the sunset; a plot so small that if you look from the inside of the house in its direction, "the window frames the whole of it," as Robert Frost said.

The only negative thing about this plot, you might say after seeing it, is its nearness to the children's play yard (the small clearing under the outer reaches of the big oak; the spot where the swing set and other items of a child's interest, have been permanently attached).

But what better place than next to a play yard to locate a graveyard, so life's whole spectrum, from first chapter to last, can be viewed at a glance.

When we first moved here, that plot was a tangle of stubborn brambles and rusty barbed wire, both with a taste for human flesh.

We spent days chopping and snatching, stacking and burning the brambles; pulling and straining, cutting and loading the wire to be hauled to the county's own wire graveyard.

The whole time we were bandaging our wounds and picking thorns from our thumbs, we never knew that this sweaty and painful undertaking was advanced preparations of sorts, like making up the bed and turning down the covers before we lay down to rest.

Even before this decision of ours, this plot had been designated as a resting place, because between a blackjack oak and a black cherry tree is where my hammock was strung (that is until the dog, during his adolescent months, tore it down, drug it off and hid most of its vitals). And while suspended between those two trees, I often thought of how I could easily spend an eternity resting while listening to the frolics of children.

This plot, it seems, has the best variety of trees for future graveyard use. Most of them shed their leaves during the cold months to allow the sunshine to trickle to the ground to form puddles of warmth across the decaying leaves that gather.

But, during the warm months, those same trees are fully clothed in green— thick and proficient at keeping out the August sun.

During that season, those treetops are loud and alive: Blue jays fussing with mocking birds and squirrels teaching their descendants how to descend and to get back to the top without waking the dog. There are ticks in the fall and old birds' nests during the winter; locusts that sing about summer weather and spring vines that run up the sides of wise old trees with gray hair of Spanish style. There are the sounds of horses and thunderstorms and train whistles sweetened by distance.

But, during the seasons to come, the most important sounds will be those of the children: those frolicking descendants in an old play yard next to an old graveyard where their ancestors rest— young laughter filling old trees, bouncing from limb to limb, until finally settling to the ground to warm and mix in a permanent fashion with remnants of past seasons here in Beulah Land.

Made in United States
Orlando, FL
07 August 2022